MW01258112

THE SEA IN YOU

Twenty Poems of Requited
and Unrequited Love

BOOKS BY DAVID WHYTE

POETRY

Songs for Coming Home
Where Many Rivers Meet
Fire in the Earth
The House of Belonging
Everything is Waiting for You
River Flow: New & Selected Poems
Pilgrim

PROSE

The Heart Aroused:
Poetry and the Preservation of the Soul
in Corporate America

Crossing the Unknown Sea:
Work as a Pilgrimage of Identity

The Three Marriages:
Reimagining Work, Self and Relationship

Consolations:
The Solace, Nourishment and Underlying Meaning
of Everyday Words

THE SEA IN YOU

*Twenty Poems of Requited
and Unrequited Love*

DAVID WHYTE

20  16

MANY RIVERS PRESS
LANGLEY WASHINGTON
www.davidwhyte.com

First published in 2016
by Many Rivers Press
PO Box 868
Langley WA 98260
USA

ISBN 978-1-932887-38-9

Printed in the United States of America

1st Printing 2016

*Dedicated
to the
sea in you.*

THE SEA IN YOU CONTENTS

THE SEA IN YOU CONTENTS *(continued)*

THE SEA IN YOU

When I wake under the moon,
I do not know who I have become unless
I move closer to you, obeying the give and take
of the earth as it breathes the slender length
of your body, so that in breathing with the tide that breathes
in you, and moving with you as you come and go,
and following you, half in light and half in dark,
I feel the first firm edge of my floating palm touch
and then trace the pale light of your shoulder
to the faint, moonlit shadow of your smooth cheek
and drawing my finger through the pearl water of your skin,
I sense the breath on your lips touch and then warm
the finest, furthest, most unknown edge of my sense of self,
so that I come to you under the moon as if I had
swum under the deepest arch of the ocean,
to find you living where no one could possibly live,
and to feel you breathing, where no one could
possibly breathe, and I touch your skin as I would
touch a pale whispering spirit of the tides that my arms
try to hold with the wrong kind of strength and my lips
try to speak with the wrong kind of love and I follow
you through the ocean night listening for your breath
in my helpless calling to love you as I should, and I lie
next to you in your sleep as I would next to the sea,
overwhelmed by the rest that arrives in me and by the weight
that is taken from me and what, by morning,
is left on the shore of my waking joy.

LOVE IN THE NIGHT

Sometimes when you lie close to me
your body is so still in my arms
I find myself half in love with your
barely breathing form and half in love
with the unspeaking silent source
from which you come. I find myself
touching your lips with mine
to feel their warmth and bowing my head
to hear your breath, and stilling myself
to listen far inside you for the gentle rise
and fall of the tide that tells me
you are still free to come and go in life,
so that I take your hand in mine to sense
your pulse and touch your hair
and stroke your cheek and move my lips
to yours to feel the warmth emerging
from your inward self and to
see we are still here and still pledged
to breathe this world together.

All night like this I find myself asleep
and awake, turned toward the moon
then turned toward you, your warmth
inviting me to bring you close
and leave you alone, all night I find myself
unable to choose between the love

I feel for you through closeness
and the grief of having to let you go
through distance, so that it seems
I can only breathe fully in the dark
by taking you in and giving you away

in your quiet rhythm of appearance
and disappearance, letting you return
only in your breathing and not breathing,
or your half-sighed phrases spoken
to the dark, whispered from the dream
in which you live, so that I lie
between sleeping and waking,
seeing you are here and dreaming you are gone,
wanting to hold you and wanting to let you go,
living far inside you as you breathe close to me,
and living far beyond you, as I wait through
the hours of the night for you to wake
and find me again, the light in your eyes
half-dreaming on the pillow
looking back at me, seeing me at last,
not knowing how far I have travelled,
through what distance I have come to find you,
where I have been, or what I have seen,
how far or how near, not knowing how
I have gained and lost you a hundred times
between darkness and dawn.

THE SEA IMAGINED

All night I lie next to you,
my body a shoreline
and yours the ocean,
your tidal presence
moving closer and then away
to return again
as some promise
made by the moon
that guides you,
breathing in and breathing out
with the living curve
of my broad chest and rising
belly, silvered by water,
my arms receiving
the entire ocean
in you and the faint brush
of your skin
like the sound of waves
always arriving and leaving,
so that I wake in the light
to a seabird's cry in my mouth,
and touch my lips to your salt neck.

SELKIE

When I held your clothes,
you ran into the sea,
and left me standing,
shocked and still,
under the sailing moon,
listening to the ocean.

When you left me alone
in your going home
you became a shiver,
a sound of laughter,
a passing glimmer
in the flowing sea.

When you left at last
and never reappeared
I knew you were a Selkie
gone back to find the water,
your spirit, whenever
I met you on the shoreline,
always half leaving, half gone,
a halfling come ashore
to test a world where a man
might touch your tidal essence,
to sense in you, some
un–imprisoned flight
to be drawn into his own depths
from which he came
to find in you, in the here
and the not here, the turn
and flow, his own unmoving,
and unbridled soul, and to touch,
in the ache of your fleeting wake,

and as surely as the growing
moon turns slowly from the
clarifying brightness of time
toward its unwanted but
necessary going,
the beginning of his own,
long feared, long sought
and long fought, disappearance.

I find, as you fade from me,
back into your immortal home,
that I arrive more fully in the
mortal world, drawn by tides of
disappearance. I find, as you
leave me, I have nothing in my hands
but sand, nothing in my ears but
the sound of the ocean
whispering your name, I find
myself able to swim in depths
I never knew until I opened those
hands and let you go. Now,
in every distance from you
I feel you ashore in me again,
as if rising from the water,
calling my original name, now I
see your hands lifted to hold me
against the bosom of time,
I sense your wet cheek against
mine, and close to me, your
familiar voice, as ever,
singing in my ears, all the ancient
and future depths of the sea.

SHORELINE

Holding hands, we walk
to the very edge of the light,
shyly aware of the way
time radiates from
where we stand.

Our footprints behind us,
are a promise in the sand,
inscribing a joining,
a walking together,
our witness to the ocean,
and as they wait
to disappear
under the flowing tide,
the far, unknown,
and unspeakable
origin from which we came.

Then, all around us,
the felt sense of a courage
needed, a newness in the air,
a touch of the familiar
and ancient in all the tidal vows
the wind can speak,
the strands of your hair
across my face, and then,
suddenly, the sun in your eyes
and the way they closed in surprise
at the first kiss of your salt mouth.

PLEDGED

Your left hand cold with rain held closely
by my ritual palms. The evening waves
tolling their Angelus on the rock below.

A cliff land of shoreline and water,
the territory in which we promise. Above,
a gull's cry as if to announce the revelation.

The cool gold slipped onto your ring finger
signals astonishment and transfiguration
and our mutual gaze moving through shyness

finds us standing together above the swaying
water, eyes giddy with the vow we utter,
and the secret nature of our understanding,

not the feeling that you had become mine, or that
I had become yours, no, in our locked eyes
some other giving away long ago, to which

we make this late testament, this recognition
and this sanctification, the ancient
and blessed origin of the waveform,
arriving with us, when we said "I do."

PEARL

The teardrop of sun that fell across the lobe
of your left ear as you turned to see me in the light

was the most perfect pearl I ever saw, no salted shell
could form it, no passing lips could ever brush its gleam

and no jeweler's window show it to the world.
No money could be earned to bring that light to you

even from the world's end, no man's riches
could ever find it in his gift to give it to you,

you wore it entirely as your own and in the fleeting
beauty of the time it took to turn your face.

Somewhere inside me is the jewel box memory
where I remember the way you speak, the way you turn

your body in the falling water, but above all
and far from you now, as I close my eyes to sleep

that moment still caught forever, deep in my heart,
when I saw you wear the priceless light.

MIDLIFE WOMAN

Midlife woman
you are not
invisible to me.
I seem to see
beneath your face
all the women
you have ever been.

Midlife woman
I have grown with you
secretly, in another parallel,
breathing with you
as you breathed,
seeing with you
as you see,
lining my face
with an earned care
as you lined yours,
waiting for you
as it seems
you waited for me.

Midlife woman
I see your
inner complexion
breathing beneath
your outward gaze,
I see all your lives
and all your loves,
it must be for you
that I wanted to become
more generous,

a better man
than ever I could be
when young,
let me join all your
present giving
and all your receiving,
through you I learn
the full imagination
of every previous affection.

Midlife woman
you are not
invisible to me,
in you
I see a young girl,
lifting her face to the sky,
I see the young woman
in haloed light,
full and strong,
standing before
the altar of time,
waiting for her chosen.
I see the mother
in you, in your past
or in some not yet
understood
future,
I see you
adoring and
I see you adored,
and now,
when I call your name

I want to see
day by day,
the woman
you will become
with me.

Midlife woman
come to me now,
I see you more clearly
than all
the airbrushed
girls of the world.
I became a warrior
only to earn
your present
mature affection,
I bear my scars to you,
my eyes are lined
to smile with you
and I come to you
uncultivated
and unshaven
walking rough
and wild through rain
and wind and I pace
the mountain
all night
in my happy,
magnificence
at finding you.

Midlife woman,
in the dark of the night
I take you in my arms
and in that embracing
invisibility feel all of your
inner lives made touchable
and visible again.

Midlife woman
I have earned
my ability to adore you.

Midlife woman
you are not invisible to me.
Come to me now
and let me kiss
passionately
all the beautiful women
who have
ever lived in you.

My promise
is to you now
and all
their future lives.

ALMOST SILENT

The almost silent rain
will heal me as it falls,
as if the sound itself
were a bed where I could lay
in your arms
letting the stream
of life
go by
unhurried
and easy
as I was with you
when
I wanted the hours
to linger on
and heaven to fall
and all the waters
of this mighty
world
run through me as
my memory of you
runs on
through my
waking body
like a spinning arrival
of weighted love
bringing me to life
this morning
and taking me
to that one night
in the grass
and ourselves
in one another

our bodies as a
burning
single
presence
and your face
becoming so familiar
so quickly to me
merely
through touch
and through the close
light
of each silvered,
midnight
glance.

Lying here
listening to the
almost
silent rain,
I hear you listening
with me
and turning
to your smiling
upturned face
I place a finger
on your
lips now
just
about to part.

To invite the quiet,
to still you with love,

to see you again;
to hear
the waters falling,
all of them
together
but
only
because I want
to whisper
next
to your ear
how glad I am,
how merciful
is life,
how good is the
night
that held us close,
realizing
how much I needed
to learn in order
to love you,
how much I was made to
wait until everything
in me was ready,
how kind life was
in keeping
you hidden
until now.

THE WHITE DOVE

When I first
wrote to you
it was as if
each letter
I held in my palms
was like
a small white
dove
I had to lift
toward the sky
and let go
and that once
it had arrived
calling
quietly
at the edge
of your high window
you only had to write
your own words
and fold them small
and tie them
to each leg
and lift
the white bird again
letting it go
into the air
as I did
so that it could
find its way
back to me and
home.

Now I find
no words
can find you
and love
has asked me
to kneel
by the window
of an
unflighted sky,
that love has
asked me
to wish you a blessing,
and to see you
gladly
on your way
as if you could
be loved
and still not mine,
and strangely
to act
in that joy
as if love were new again;
calling me
to its sweet side,
as if,
after all
these words,
words will never do,
and in the still air
where words
cannot reach
and where I found

you before
you have become
the white dove now,

and the one
I must lift
in the air
and let go.

LARK SONG AND LETTING GO

Lark song and your face above me in the clouds,
lark song and your face carried away from me,
lark song and letting you go in the great river
of the sky, mightier than my love's power to hold you.

My heart melted with the first fall of notes
from the tiny mouth
of the calling, ascending, windblown bird.

Lark song and my own brave sung lament
joined with it, reformed in the music of the wind
saying, I will love and lose again,
and lose and still love again. The word *Always,*
carried as a promise in the wind.

You made me make promises
but now I will make them
with or without you,
because of you, I am larger, braver, and able
to see my lone outline against the sky
because of you I am made raw and beautiful
in the world's eyes, brought to earth
and then raised through powers
I learned in loving you, to fly again.

You have taught me the keen humiliations
of the rain and the wind you have led
me into the dark, crowding, cloud-filled horizon,
you have shown me the lonely walk
I must take through high mountain grass.
You have led me by falling waters speaking with me
as we walk together invisibly and now I walk

in parallel with your future self
walking with me as you leave to go,
and I cast a blessing before you,
May the gift you have given me
return from every path you take.

You turn, to look back and smile,
to see me standing strong
and unashamed, head held high,
smiling to wave you on
a readiness in my eyes,
a looking still, for you and me:
but it's you in your safe journey now,
you going onward, you with your head
turned away and me, me watching you go,
and just about to go somewhere too,
my eyes ready to see
as I have been taught to see,
my horizon and your horizon
open and freed from being together.

COURAGE AND BEAUTY

Your beauty
is in your courage
and your courage
in the way
you risk your beauty
in the world,
and then shyly
through your moving grace
the way you dance
from place to place.

Your nobility
is in your face
turned to me,
and then away,
a sweep of fair hair
and fly-away tress
and the hidden,
elegant current
that trembles
your silk dress.

I do not think I can bear
to harm the dancer in you
by wanting to circle
with unseemly haste
this clumsy hand
round your slender waist.

I do not think
I can follow you
where you want to go,

in the arms
of beautiful strangers
beneath the dance floor lights
holding you close
under the arch
of distant nights.

I turn beneath
the light starred sky
and leave the floor
and walk a lonely way
to the silvered waiting door
and after the shiver
and hesitation
of one last turn to see,
I wave unseen,
walk quickly
through,
and set you free.

IN A MOMENT OF MADNESS,
A DUBLIN POET THINKS OF
AN OLD LOVE

Twenty years since I knew her.
Wherever she is now, I will go to her.
I know you can never believe me
but her face is as fresh to me
as the winter day we parted.

Once my life was like a flight
through clear air, searching the field lines
for a high place from which to see.
Now they have clipped my wings,
turned my proud eagle flight
into the hesitant perching of a shivering wren.

It is in the shape of my old self then,
the hawk, the curlew, or anything wild
that flies against the sky
that I'll find her once again,
staring out from the woods
of a winter evening.

Like this then,
as a soundless shadow of love,
I will fly to the low branch above her.

SEPTEMBER

I said goodbye and still you would not go,
you turned smiling to look at me as you stood
with your hand rested lightly on the head
of our imaginary child. You smiled at me, saying–
Everything you saw and heard me say in the lighted day
was not true, out of my unknowing I must go away
and enter that familiar dark where everything began.

I will come and find you when the love
I find inside myself is equal to what you offer,
I have been so afraid in that outer world
in which you found me; one thing I know
that I do not need to ask you to wait.
I only want to tell you that here in the center
of my strength I am everything you have seen.
I will come in late September when the light
inside me and outside of me has utterly changed.
All of this will come true.

MUSE

The words insistent, wishing to be said,
I walk back to the house, find the room lit,
a woman illuminated, by a table with flowers,
needle in hand, her long fingers threading the cloth
with dark red thread. She turns to look.

The house is quiet, the wind shivers behind me,
there is a single drop of blood on her hand.

THE FOX

I remember the fox
and your train to the east,
two travellers, secret, alone
in mutual recognition
of the eyes, the ears,
the wild red fur,
and after, your look of surprise
at the sudden, tawny flash
across the road,
our knowing then,
in the fox, our journey
our way forward, our parting,
and our instincts already like him,
fugitive, glimpsed, at bay,
his fleeting a preparation
for you to go on
into what you loved, your
arrival in my life
so sudden and then
so quickly, through
the misted moving window,
your red–gold hair and
your final disappearance.

THE HAWTHORN

The crossed knot
in the hawthorn bark
and the stump
of the sawn off branch
hemmed by
the roughened trunk.
In that
omniscient black eye
of witness
I see the dark no-growth
of what has passed
grown round by
what has come to pass,
looking at me
as if I could speak.

So much that was
good in her,
so much in me,
cut off now
from the future
in which we
grew together.

Now
through the window
of my new house
that hawthorn's
crooked faithful
trunk round
an old and broken
growth,

my mouth dumb
and
Dante's voice
instead of mine
from the open book.

Brother, our love
has laid our wills to rest.
Making us long
only for what is ours
and by no other thirst
possessed.

Our life not lived
together
must still
live on apart,
longing only
for what is ours
alone,
each grow
round the missed branch
as best we can,
claim what is ours
separately,
though not forget
loved memories,
nor that life
still loved by memory,
nor the hurts
through which we

hesitantly
tried to learn
affection.

Our pilgrim journey
apart or together,
like the thirst
of everything
to find its true form,
the grain of the wood
round the hatched knot
still straightening
toward the light.

LIVING TOGETHER

We are like children in the master's violin shop
not yet allowed to touch the tiny planes or the rare wood
but given brooms to sweep the farthest corners
of the room, to gather shavings, mop spilled resins
and watch with apprehension the tender curves
emerging from apprenticed hands. The master
rarely shows himself but whenever he does he demonstrates
a concentrated ease so different from the willful accumulation
of experience we have come to expect,
a stripping away, a direct appreciation of all the elements
we are bound, one day, to find beneath our hands.
He stands in our minds so clearly now, his confident back
caught in the light from pale clerestory windows
and we note the way the slight tremor of his palms
disappears the moment they encounter wood.

In this light we hunger for maturity, see it not as stasis
but a form of love. We want the stillness and confidence
of age, the space between self and all the objects of the world
honoured and defined, the possibility that everything
left alone can ripen of its own accord,
all passionate transformations arranged only
through innocent meetings, one to another,
the way we see resin allowed to seep into the wood
in the wood's own secret time. We intuit our natures
becoming resonant with one another according
to the grain of the way we are made. Nothing forced
or wanted until it ripens in our own expectant hands.
But for now, in the busy room, we stand in the child's
first shy witness of one another, and see ourselves again,
gladly and always, falling in love with our future.

THE TRUELOVE

There is a faith in loving fiercely
the one who is rightfully yours
especially if you have
waited years and especially
if part of you never believed
you could deserve this
loved and beckoning hand
held out to you this way.

I am thinking of faith now
and the testaments of loneliness
and what we feel we are
worthy of in this world.

Years ago in the Hebrides
I remember an old man
who walked every morning
on the grey stones
to the shore of baying seals
who would press his hat
to his chest in the blustering
salt wind and say his prayer
to the turbulent Jesus
hidden in the water,

and I think of the story
of the storm and everyone
waking and seeing
the distant
yet familiar figure

far across the water
calling to them

and how we are all
preparing for that
abrupt waking,
and that calling,
and that moment
we have to say yes,
except it will
not come so grandly
so Biblically
but more subtly
and intimately in the face
of the one you know
you have to love.

So that when
we finally step out of the boat
toward them, we find
everything holds
us, and everything confirms
our courage, and if you wanted
to drown you could,
but you don't
because finally
after all this struggle
and all these years
you don't want to any more
you've simply had enough
of drowning

and you want to live and you
want to love and you will
walk across any territory
and any darkness
however fluid and however
dangerous to take the
one hand you know
belongs in yours.

STONE
(Thobar Phádraig)

The face in the stone is a mirror looking into you.
You have gazed into the moving waters,
you have seen the slow light, in the sky
above Lough Inagh, beneath you, streams have flowed,
and rivers of earth have moved beneath your feet,
but you have never looked into the immovability
of stone like this, the way it holds you, gives you
not a way forward but a doorway in, staunches
your need to leave, becomes faithful by going nowhere,
something that wants you to stay here and look back,
be weathered by what comes to you, like the way you too
have travelled from so far away to be here, once reluctant
and now as solid and as here and as willing
to be touched as everything you have found.

TO BREAK A PROMISE
(Cúnga Fheichin)

Make a place of prayer, no fuss,
just lean into the white brilliance
and say what you needed to say
all along, nothing too much, words
as simple and as yours and as heard
as the birdsong above your head
or the river running gently beside you.

Let the words join
one to another
the way stone nestles on stone,
the way water just leaves
and goes to the sea,
the way your promise
breathes and belongs
with every other promise
the world has ever made.

Now, leave them to go on,
let your words
carry their own life,
without you, let the promise
go with the river.
Have faith. Walk away.

INTO THIN AIR
(Cathair an Ard Rois)

Some day
take the road above
to Caher Anadurrish,
when you've taken
that miracle hour alone,

so that below you
the green valley is filled
from end to end
with whitethorn
and birdsong

while above,
the blue moving sky
is torn
by wind and cloud

and following the road
to the very top
looking to neither
left nor right
keep going
as if you could walk
straight off
into that horizon,
and on
into the thin air
of your waiting life.

Into the future
your ancestors,
working
the rock of the land
might have wanted
you to have,

into the past
you might deny
has brought you here

and into the promise
far inside you
trying to break out
and meet the sky.

All the airy nothings
you thought
would never
hold your weight.

The sense
of beckoning newness,
the lightness of air.

And you,
in that miracle hour
afraid only
in some inward part
that

doesn't matter
any more,
walking on
through
the beckoning sky.

LEAVING THE ISLAND
(Inishbofin)

It must have been
the slant of the light,
the sheer cross-grain of rain
against the summer sun,
the way the island appeared
gifted, out of the gleam
and the depth of distance,
so that when you turned
to look again,
the scend of the sea
had carried you on,
through veils of rain,
into the waiting harbour.

And after the pilgrim lanes,
and the ruined chapel,
the gull cries and the sea-hush
at the back of the island,
it was the way, standing still
or looking out
or walking or even talking
with others in the evening bar,
holding your drink
or laughing with the rest,
that you realized part of you
had already dropped to its knees,
to pray, to sing, to look,
to fall in love with everything
and everyone again,
that someone from far inside you

had walked out into the sea light
to raise its hands
and forgive
everyone in your short life
you thought you hadn't,
and that all along
you had been singing
your quiet way
through the rosary of silence
that held their names.

Above all, the way afterwards,
you thought you had left the island
but hadn't, the way you knew
you had gone somewhere
into the shimmering light
and come out again on the tide
as you knew you had to,
as someone who would return
and live in the world again,
a man granted just a glimpse,
someone half a shade braver,
a standing silhouette in the stern,
holding the rail,
riding the long waves back,
ready for the exile we call a home.

For more about David Whyte's work, including his walking tours, public speaking engagements and work with organizations:

MANY RIVERS
PO Box 868
Langley WA 98260
USA

360.221.1324
www.davidwhyte.com
mrivers@davidwhyte.com